MASTERING MO[...]
REACT

BUILD DYNAMIC AND ENGAGING CHARTS

OLIVER LUCAS JR

Preface

In the ever-evolving landscape of web development, React has emerged as a dominant force, empowering developers to build dynamic and interactive user interfaces. And within this vibrant ecosystem, data visualization plays a crucial role in transforming raw data into meaningful insights. This book, "Mastering Modern React: Build Dynamic and Engaging Charts," serves as your comprehensive guide to harnessing the power of React for creating compelling and informative data visualizations.

Whether you're a seasoned React developer or just starting your journey, this book will equip you with the knowledge and skills to craft a wide range of charts, from basic line and bar charts to more complex visualizations like stacked area charts and interactive scatter plots. We'll delve into the core concepts of React, explore popular charting libraries like Recharts, and guide you through essential techniques for data handling, customization, and optimization.

This book goes beyond simply presenting code examples. We'll delve into the "why" behind the techniques, providing you with a deeper understanding of how to choose the right chart types, customize their appearance, and ensure they are accessible and performant. You'll learn how to:

Master fundamental React concepts: JSX, components, props, and state.

Leverage the power of Recharts: Create various chart types, customize their appearance, and add interactivity.

Handle data effectively: Fetch data from APIs, transform and prepare it for visualization, and manage dynamic updates.

Optimize for performance: Implement lazy loading, code splitting, and other techniques to ensure smooth rendering.

Build real-world applications: Create dashboards, data exploration tools, and real-time visualizations.

Explore advanced libraries: Integrate D3.js for custom visualizations and add animations with Framer Motion and React Spring.

Throughout this journey, we'll emphasize best practices for creating accessible and user-friendly charts that effectively communicate data-driven insights. By the end of this book, you'll be well-equipped to tackle any data visualization challenge with confidence and creativity.

So, let's embark on this exciting journey to master the art of building dynamic and engaging charts with React. Get ready to transform data into compelling visual stories!

TABLE OF CONTENTS

Chapter 4

4.1 Interactive Charts (Tooltips, zooming, panning) - Code examples: adding tooltips to a line chart, implementing zoom and pan functionality
4.2 Animations and Transitions (Making charts visually appealing) - Code examples: animating chart elements on data updates, transitions for smooth rendering
4.3 Customizing Chart Appearance (Colors, fonts, legends) - Code examples: styling chart elements with CSS, creating custom legends

Chapter 5

5.1 Fetching Data from APIs (REST APIs, asynchronous requests) - Code examples: using fetch to retrieve data, handling loading states
5.2 Data Transformation and Preparation (Filtering, sorting, aggregation) - Code examples: using JavaScript array methods to prepare data for charts
5.3 State Management for Chart Data (Updating charts dynamically) - Code examples: using React state to update chart data, handling user interactions

Chapter 6

Chapter 7

Chapter 8

Chapter 9

Chapter 10

10.1 Exploring Advanced Libraries (D3.js for custom visualizations) - Code examples: basic D3.js integration, creating custom chart elements

10.2 Creating Animated Charts with Libraries (Framer Motion, React Spring) - Code examples: animating chart elements with Framer Motion, creating spring animations

10.3 Building Reusable Chart Components (Creating a library of custom chart components) - Code examples: building a reusable bar chart component, creating a chart component library

Chapter 1

Introduction to React and Data Visualization

1.1 Why React for Charts? (Benefits, ecosystem, etc.)

React has become a dominant force in front-end web development, and it's an excellent choice for building dynamic and engaging charts. Here's why:

1. Component-Based Architecture:

Reusability: React's core strength lies in its component-based structure. You can create reusable chart components for different chart types (line, bar, pie, etc.) or even specific parts of a chart (legends, axes, tooltips). This modularity promotes code organization, maintainability, and efficiency.

Flexibility: Components are like building blocks. You can compose complex charts by combining simpler ones, allowing you to create highly customized and intricate visualizations.

Maintainability: When you need to update a chart's functionality or styling, you only need to modify the relevant component. This isolation makes it easier to manage and debug your code.

2. Rich Ecosystem:

Powerful Charting Libraries: React has a thriving ecosystem of charting libraries that provide pre-built components, utilities, and APIs for creating various types of charts. Popular options include:

Recharts: A composable charting library built on top of SVG elements, known for its simplicity and flexibility.

Chart.js: A versatile library with a wide range of chart types and customization options.

D3.js: A powerful library for creating custom and highly interactive visualizations.

Victory: A collection of composable React components for building data visualizations with a focus on mobile responsiveness.

Community Support: The large and active React community ensures ample resources, tutorials, and support for developers working with charts.

3. Performance:

Virtual DOM: React's virtual DOM efficiently updates only the necessary parts of the actual DOM when data changes, minimizing expensive browser rendering operations. This is crucial for charts, which often involve dynamic updates and animations.

Optimization Techniques: React provides tools and techniques for optimizing performance, such as memoization and code splitting, to ensure smooth and responsive chart interactions.

4. Declarative Style:

Simplified Development: React's declarative style allows you to describe how your charts should look based on the data. This makes the code easier to read, understand, and reason about, especially when dealing with complex visualizations.

Reduced Complexity: You don't need to manually manipulate the DOM to update your charts. React handles the rendering logic, allowing you to focus on the data and the desired outcome.

5. Integration with Other Technologies:

Data Fetching: React seamlessly integrates with libraries and APIs for fetching data from various sources, including REST APIs,

GraphQL endpoints, and real-time data streams. This is essential for creating data-driven charts.

State Management: React works well with state management libraries like Redux and Zustand, which help manage and update the data that drives your charts.

In summary: React's component-based architecture, rich ecosystem, performance optimizations, declarative style, and seamless integration with other technologies make it an ideal choice for building dynamic, interactive, and engaging charts for modern web applications.

1.2 Setting Up Your Development Environment (Node.js, npm, create-react-app)

1. Install Node.js and npm:

Download: Go to the official Node.js website (nodejs.org) and download the LTS (Long-Term Support) version for your operating system. This will also install npm (Node Package Manager), which is essential for managing project dependencies.

Verify Installation: Open your terminal or command prompt and run the following commands to check if Node.js and npm are installed correctly:

Bash

```
node -v
npm -v
```

These commands should display the installed versions of Node.js and npm.

2. Install Create React App:

Create React App is a command-line tool that sets up a new React project with a pre-configured development environment. It handles all the complex configurations, allowing you to focus on building your application.

Install Globally (Optional): While not required, installing it globally can be convenient. Use the following command:

Bash

```
npm install -g create-react-app
```

3. Create a New React Project:

Navigate to Project Directory: Open your terminal and navigate to the directory where you want to create your project.

Create the App: Use `create-react-app` to generate a new project:

Bash

```
npx create-react-app my-chart-app
```

(Replace `my-chart-app` with your desired project name)

This command will:

Create a new folder with your project name.

Set up a basic React project structure.

Install all the necessary dependencies.

4. Start the Development Server:

Navigate to Project Folder: Once the project is created, navigate into the project directory:

Bash

```bash
cd my-chart-app
```

Start the Server: Run the following command to start the development server:

Bash

```bash
npm start
```

This will:

Start a local development server.

Open your React application in your default web browser (usually at `http://localhost:3000`).

Automatically reload the browser whenever you make changes to your code.

5. Project Structure:

`node_modules`: Contains all the project's dependencies (packages installed via npm).

`public`: Stores static files like `index.html` (the main HTML file) and any images or other assets.

`src`: This is where you'll write most of your React code. It typically contains:

`index.js` : The entry point of your application.

`App.js`: The main component of your application.

You're now ready to start building your React charting application! This setup provides a solid foundation for developing and running your React projects. If you have any issues during the setup process, refer to the official Create React App documentation for troubleshooting and more detailed information.

1.3 Fundamental React Concepts (JSX, components, props, state) - Code examples: basic component structure, rendering data with JSX

Okay, let's break down those fundamental React concepts with code examples!

1. JSX (JavaScript XML)

What it is: JSX is a syntax extension to JavaScript that allows you to write HTML-like code within your JavaScript files. It makes your React code more readable and easier to work with.

Example:

JavaScript

```
const element = <h1>Hello, world!</h1>;
```

This JSX code represents an `<h1>` heading element. React will take this JSX and convert it into regular JavaScript code that the browser can understand.

Embedding Expressions: You can embed JavaScript expressions within JSX using curly braces { }.

JavaScript

```
const name = 'John Doe';
const element = <h1>Hello, {name}</h1>;
```

This will render "Hello, John Doe" in the browser.

2. Components

What they are: Components are the building blocks of React applications. They are reusable pieces of code that encapsulate a specific part of the user interface (UI).

Example:

JavaScript

```
function Welcome(props) {
   return <h1>Hello, {props.name}</h1>;
}
```

This defines a functional component called `Welcome` that takes a `props` object as input and returns a JSX element.

Rendering a component:

JavaScript

```
ReactDOM.render(
   <Welcome name="Sarah" />,
   document.getElementById('root')
);
```

This line of code renders the `Welcome` component with the `name` prop set to "Sarah" into the HTML element with the ID "root."

3. Props

What they are: Props (short for "properties") are a way to pass data from a parent component to a child component. They are read-only within the child component.

Example (using the `Welcome` component from above):

JavaScript

```
<Welcome name="Alice" />
```

Here, we are passing the string "Alice" as the value for the `name` prop to the `Welcome` component.

4. State

What it is: State is data that is internal to a component and can be changed over time. When state changes, the component re-renders to reflect the updated data.

Example:

JavaScript

```
function Counter() {
  const [count, setCount] = useState(0);

  return (
    <div>
      <p>You clicked {count} times</p>
```

```
      <button onClick={() => setCount(count +
1)}>
        Click me
      </button>
    </div>[1]
  );
}
```

This `Counter` component uses the `useState` Hook to manage its internal state (`count`). Clicking the button updates the `count` state, causing the component to re-render and display the new count.

Key Takeaways

JSX lets you write HTML-like code in your JavaScript.

Components are reusable UI units.

Props pass data down from parent to child components.

State manages internal component data that can change.

These fundamental concepts are the foundation for building any React application. Understanding them well will help you create dynamic and interactive user interfaces with ease.

Chapter 2

Working with Charting Libraries

2.1 Overview of Popular Libraries (Recharts, Chart.js, D3.js)

Let's dive into those popular React charting libraries!

1. Recharts

Overview: Recharts is a composable charting library built on top of D3.js and designed specifically for React applications. It offers a declarative approach to creating charts using reusable React components.

Key Features:

Composability: Build complex charts by combining smaller, simpler components (e.g., `<LineChart>`, `<XAxis>`, `<YAxis>`, `<Tooltip>`).

Declarative Syntax: Define charts using JSX, making the code more readable and maintainable.

Native SVG Support: Renders charts using SVG, providing crisp visuals and scalability.

Customization: Offers a wide range of customization options for styling and interactivity.

Lightweight: Relatively small bundle size compared to some other libraries.

Best for: Developers who want a React-specific library with a simple API and good performance for common chart types.

2. Chart.js

Overview: Chart.js is a versatile and popular JavaScript charting library that works well with React. It provides a wide variety of chart types and customization options.

Key Features:

Variety of Chart Types: Supports a comprehensive range of chart types, including line, bar, pie, doughnut, scatter, bubble, radar, and more.

Responsive Design: Charts automatically adjust to different screen sizes.

Animations: Provides built-in animations for dynamic chart updates.

Easy to Use: Relatively simple API for creating and customizing charts.

Good Documentation: Extensive documentation and examples are available.

Best for: Developers who need a wide range of chart types and prioritize ease of use and customization.

3. D3.js

Overview: D3.js (Data-Driven Documents) is a powerful JavaScript library for creating custom and highly interactive data visualizations. It provides complete control over the rendering process using web standards (SVG, HTML, CSS).

Key Features:

Flexibility: Offers unparalleled flexibility for creating unique and complex visualizations.

Data Binding: Powerful data binding capabilities for connecting data to visual elements.

Animations and Transitions: Extensive support for creating smooth and engaging animations.

Large Community: A massive and active community provides abundant resources and support.

Best for: Developers who need maximum control over their visualizations and are comfortable working with a lower-level library.

Choosing the Right Library

Project Requirements: Consider the specific needs of your project, including the types of charts, level of customization, and performance requirements.

React Integration: Recharts is specifically designed for React, while Chart.js and D3.js can be integrated with React but might require some additional configuration.

Learning Curve: Recharts is generally easier to learn, while D3.js has a steeper learning curve due to its flexibility and lower-level API.

Community and Support: All three libraries have active communities, but D3.js has the largest and most established community.

By understanding the strengths and weaknesses of each library, you can choose the best one for your React charting project.

2.2 Choosing the Right Library for Your Project (Considerations and comparisons)

You're absolutely right to emphasize the importance of choosing the right charting library. It can significantly impact your project's success. Here's a breakdown of key considerations and comparisons to help you make an informed decision:

1. Project Requirements:

Chart Types:

Recharts: Excellent for common chart types (line, bar, area, pie, scatter).

Chart.js: Offers the widest range of chart types, including more specialized ones (radar, polar area, etc.).

D3.js: Can create any chart imaginable, but requires more effort for standard types.

- **Customization:**

Recharts: Good customization within its predefined components, but can be limiting for highly unique designs.

Chart.js: Extensive configuration options for appearance, animations, and interactions.

D3.js: Ultimate flexibility for creating completely custom visualizations.

Interactivity:

All three: Support interactive features like tooltips, zooming, and panning.D3.js offers the finest level of control over interactions.

Performance:

Recharts: Generally performs well due to its React-specific optimizations.

Chart.js: Can handle moderate datasets efficiently.

D3.js: Performance depends heavily on implementation; can be highly optimized but requires careful coding.

2. Development Experience:

React Proficiency:

Recharts: Ideal if you're comfortable with React's component-based model and JSX.

Chart.js: Requires some React knowledge for integration.

D3.js: React experience is helpful but not mandatory; focuses more on data visualization concepts.

Learning Curve:

Recharts: Easiest to learn, with a clear API and good documentation.

Chart.js: Relatively easy to pick up, especially with its extensive examples.

D3.js: Steeper learning curve due to its lower-level API and focus on data manipulation.

3. Ecosystem and Support:

Community:

D3.js: Largest and most mature community, with abundant resources and tutorials.

Chart.js: Active community with good documentation and support.

Recharts: Growing community, with decent documentation and support.

Third-Party Tools:

Recharts: Integrates well with other React libraries and tools.

Chart.js: Has a large number of plugins and extensions.

D3.js: A vast ecosystem of tools and libraries built around it.

Here's a quick comparison table:

Feature	Recharts	Chart.js	D3.js
React Integration	Excellent	Good	Requires wrappers/integration
Chart Types	Common types	Wide range	Unlimited
Customization	Good	Extensive	Maximum
Learning Curve	Easy	Moderate	Steep
Performance	Good	Good	Variable
Community	Growing	Active	Largest

Ultimately, the best choice depends on your project's specific needs and your priorities as a developer.

If you're building a React application and need common chart types with good performance and ease of use, Recharts is an excellent option. If you require a wider variety of charts or more extensive customization, Chart.js is a strong contender. For maximum control and the ability to create highly specialized visualizations, D3.js is the way to go.

2.3 Installing and Importing Libraries - Code examples: installing Recharts, basic chart rendering with Recharts

1. Installing Recharts

You'll need npm (Node Package Manager) or yarn to install Recharts. Open your terminal and run one of the following commands:

Bash

```
# Using npm

npm install recharts


# Using yarn

yarn add recharts
```

This will download the Recharts library and add it to your project's `node_modules` folder.

2. Importing Recharts Components

In your React component file, import the necessary components from Recharts. Here's a basic example where we import `LineChart`, `Line`, `XAxis`, `YAxis`, and `Tooltip`:

JavaScript

```javascript
import React from 'react';

import { LineChart, Line, XAxis, YAxis, Tooltip }
from 'recharts';
```

3. Preparing Your Data

Recharts expects data in a specific format, usually an array of objects. Each object represents a data point and should have keys that correspond to the values you want to display on the chart. Here's an example:

JavaScript

```javascript
const data = [

    { name: 'Page A', uv: 4000, pv: 2400, amt: 2400
},

    { name: 'Page B', uv: 3000, pv: 1398, amt: 2210
},

    { name: 'Page C', uv: 2000, pv: 9800, amt: 2290
},

    { name: 'Page D', uv: 2780, pv: 3908, amt: 2000
},

    { name: 'Page E', uv: 1890, pv: 4800, amt: 2181
},

    { name: 'Page F', uv: 2390, pv: 3800, amt: 2500
},

    { name: 'Page G', uv: 3490, pv: 4300, amt: 2100
},
```

```
];
```

4. Rendering a Basic Chart

Now, let's create a simple line chart using the imported components and data:

JavaScript

```javascript
function MyLineChart() {

  return (

        <LineChart  width={500}  height={300}
data={data}>

    <XAxis dataKey="name" />

    <YAxis />

    <Tooltip />

        <Line  type="monotone"  dataKey="uv"
stroke="#8884d8" />

    </LineChart>

  );

}
```

Explanation:

`<LineChart>`: The main component that wraps the chart. We set the `width`, `height`, and provide the `data`.

`<XAxis>`: Renders the horizontal axis. `dataKey="name"` specifies that the `name` property from our data array will be used for the axis labels.

`<YAxis>`: Renders the vertical axis.

`<Tooltip>`: Displays information about data points when hovered over.

`<Line>`: Creates a line series on the chart. `dataKey="uv"` indicates that the `uv` property from our data will determine the line's values, and `stroke` sets the line color.

5. Rendering the Chart Component

Finally, render your `MyLineChart` component in your main app component (e.g., `App.js`):

JavaScript

```javascript
import React from 'react';

import MyLineChart from './MyLineChart'; // Assuming MyLineChart is in the same directory


function App() {

  return (

    <div>

      <MyLineChart />

    </div>

  );

}
```

```
export default App;
```

This will display a basic line chart in your React application. You can further customize the chart's appearance, add more data series, and include interactive elements using other Recharts components and props.

Chapter 3

Building Basic Charts

3.1 Creating Line Charts (Data formatting, customization) - Code examples: simple line chart with Recharts, customizing axes and labels

1. Data Formatting

Recharts expects data in an array of objects. Each object represents a data point on your line chart. The properties of these objects will be used to determine the position and values on the chart.

Example:

JavaScript

```javascript
const data = [

  { date: '2024-11-20', value: 120 },

  { date: '2024-11-21', value: 150 },

  { date: '2024-11-22', value: 130 },

  { date: '2024-11-23', value: 180 },

  { date: '2024-11-24', value: 160 },

];
```

Key Considerations:

Consistency: Ensure your data types are consistent (e.g., dates should be in a consistent format like 'YYYY-MM-DD').

`dataKey`: You'll use the `dataKey` prop in Recharts components to specify which property from your data objects should be used for the x-axis (`XAxis`) and y-axis (`YAxis`).

2. Simple Line Chart Example

JavaScript

```
import React from 'react';

import { LineChart, Line, XAxis, YAxis,
CartesianGrid, Tooltip, Legend } from 'recharts';


const data¹ = [ /* ... your data as shown above
... */ ];


function MyLineChart() {

  return (

        <LineChart width={600} height={300}
data={data}

      margin={{ top: 5, right: 30, left: 20,
bottom: 5 }}>

    <XAxis dataKey="date" />

    <YAxis />

    <CartesianGrid strokeDasharray="3 3" />
```

```
    <Tooltip />

    <Legend[2] />

        <Line  type="monotone"  dataKey="value"
stroke="#8884d8" />

    </LineChart>

  );

}




export default[3] MyLineChart;
```

3. Customizing Axes and Labels

XAxis Customization:

JavaScript

```
<XAxis

  dataKey="date"

        label={{    value:    'Date',    position:
'insideBottomRight', offset: 0 }}

  tickFormatter={(date) => {

    // Format the date (e.g., 'Nov 20')

                            return           new
Date(date).toLocaleDateString('en-US',  {  month:
'short', day: 'numeric' });
```

```
  }}

/>
```

YAxis Customization:

JavaScript

```
<YAxis

  label={{ value: 'Value', angle: -90, position:
'insideLeft' }}

  tickFormatter={(value) => `${value} units`}

/>
```

Explanation:

`label`: Adds a label to the axis. You can customize its `value`, `position`, `angle` (for Y-axis), and `offset`.

`tickFormatter`: A function that lets you format the tick labels on the axis. In the example, we format the date and add "units" to the y-axis values.

4. More Customization Options

Line Customization:

`stroke`: Change the line color.

`strokeWidth`: Adjust the line thickness.

`type`: Specify the line type (e.g., `monotone`, `step`, `linear`).

`dot`: Customize or disable data point markers.

Chart Area:

`margin`: Add margins around the chart area.

`<CartesianGrid>`: Customize the grid lines with `stroke`, `strokeDasharray`.

By combining these customization options, you can create line charts that effectively represent your data and match your application's design. Remember to refer to the Recharts documentation for a complete list of props and customization possibilities.

3.2 Building Bar Charts (Categorical data, styling) - Code examples: basic bar chart, grouped bar chart

1. Categorical Data

Bar charts are excellent for visualizing categorical data, where you have distinct groups or categories and want to compare their values. Your data should be structured as an array of objects, where each object represents a category and its corresponding value.

Example:

JavaScript

```
const data = [
  { name: 'Category A', value: 40 },
  { name: 'Category B', value: 70 },
  { name: 'Category C', value: 30 },
  { name: 'Category D', value: 90 },
```

```
  { name: 'Category E', value: 60 },

];
```

2. Basic Bar Chart Example

JavaScript

```javascript
import React from 'react';

import { BarChart, Bar, XAxis, YAxis,
CartesianGrid, Tooltip, Legend } from 'recharts';


const data = [ /* ... your data as shown above
... */ ];


function MyBarChart() {

  return (

          <BarChart  width={600}  height={300}
data={data}>

      <XAxis dataKey="name" />

      <YAxis />

      <CartesianGrid strokeDasharray="3 3" />

      <Tooltip />

      <Legend />

      <Bar dataKey="value"[1] fill="#8884d8" />
```

```
    </BarChart>²

  );

}


export default MyBarChart;
```

Explanation:

`<BarChart>`: The main component for creating a bar chart.

`<Bar>`: Renders the bars. `dataKey="value"` specifies that the `value` property from the data will determine the bar heights. `fill` sets the color of the bars.

3. Grouped Bar Chart Example

To create a grouped bar chart, you'll need multiple `<Bar>` components with different `dataKey` values and `fill` colors.

JavaScript

```
import React from 'react';

import { BarChart, Bar, XAxis, YAxis,
CartesianGrid, Tooltip, Legend } from 'recharts';


const data = [

  { name: 'Category³ A', value1: 40, value2: 60
},

  { name: 'Category B', value1: 70, value2: 30 },
```

```
  { name: 'Category C', value1: 30, value2: 80 },

  { name: 'Category D', value1: 90, value2: 50 },

  { name: 'Category E', value1: 60, value2: 70 },

];


function MyGroupedBarChart() {

  return (

        <BarChart  width={600}  height={300}
data={data}>

    <XAxis dataKey="name" />

    <YAxis />

    <CartesianGrid strokeDasharray="3 3" />

    <Tooltip />

    <Legend />

    <Bar dataKey="value1"⁴ fill="#8884d8" />

    <Bar dataKey="value2" fill="#82ca9d" />

  </BarChart>

  );

}


export default MyGroupedBarChart;
```

4. Styling Bar Charts

Recharts provides various options for styling bar charts:

Bar Properties:

`fill`: Sets the fill color of the bars.

`stroke`: Adds a stroke (border) to the bars.

`strokeWidth`: Adjusts the stroke width.

`barSize`: Controls the width of the bars.

`radius`: Adds rounded corners to the bars.

Chart Area:

`margin`: Adds margins around the chart.

`<CartesianGrid>`: Customizes the grid lines.

Axes and Labels:

Customize axes and labels as shown in the previous example (using `label` and `tickFormatter`).

5. Advanced Styling

For more advanced styling, you can:

Use CSS: Apply CSS classes to chart elements for further customization.

Custom `Tooltip` Content: Create custom tooltip content to display more detailed information.

Add Labels to Bars: Use the `<LabelList>` component to add labels to the bars.

By exploring these styling options, you can create visually appealing and informative bar charts that effectively communicate your data. Remember to consult the Recharts documentation for a complete list of styling props and examples.

3.3 Pie Charts and Doughnut Charts (Proportional data representation) - Code examples: pie chart with labels, customized doughnut chart

1. Data for Pie and Doughnut Charts

Pie and doughnut charts are effective for displaying the proportions of different categories within a whole. The data should be an array of objects, where each object represents a category and its value.

Example:

JavaScript

```
const data = [
  { name: 'Category A', value: 40 },
  { name: 'Category B', value: 30 },
  { name: 'Category C', value: 20 },
  { name: 'Category D', value: 10 },
];
```

2. Pie Chart with Labels

JavaScript

```javascript
import React from 'react';

import { PieChart, Pie, Cell, Legend, Label }
from 'recharts';


const data = [ /* ... your data as shown above
... */ ];


const COLORS = ['#0088FE', '#00C49F', '#FFBB28',
'#FF8042'];


function MyPieChart() {

  return (

    <PieChart width={400} height={400}>

      <Legend />

      <Pie

        data={data}

        cx={200} // Center x-coordinate

        cy={200} // Center y-coordinate

          innerRadius={60} // Inner radius for a
doughnut-like effect (optional)
```

```jsx
          outerRadius={100}

          fill="#8884d8"

          dataKey="value"

          label // Display labels on the slices
        >

          {data.map((entry, index) => (
                      <Cell  key={`cell-${index}`}
fill={COLORS[index % COLORS.length]} />

          ))}

                      <Label  value="Categories"
position="center" />

      </Pie>

    </PieChart>

  );

}



export default MyPieChart;
```

Explanation:

`<PieChart>`: The main component for pie charts.

`<Pie>`: Renders the pie.

cx and cy: Define the center coordinates of the pie.

innerRadius and outerRadius: Control the size of the pie. Set innerRadius to create a doughnut chart.

dataKey: Specifies the property from the data that determines the slice sizes.

label: Enables labels on the slices.

<Cell>: Allows customizing the color of each slice.

<Label>: Adds a label to the center of the pie.

3. Customized Doughnut Chart

JavaScript

```javascript
import React from 'react';

import { PieChart, Pie, Sector } from 'recharts';


const data = [ /* ... your data as shown above ... */ ];


const renderActiveShape = (props) => {

  const RADIAN = Math.PI / 180;

    const { cx, cy, midAngle, innerRadius, outerRadius, startAngle, endAngle, fill, payload, percent, value } = props;

  const sin = Math.sin(-RADIAN * midAngle);
```

```
const cos = Math.cos(-RADIAN * midAngle);

const sx = cx + (outerRadius + 10) * cos;

const sy = cy + (outerRadius + 10) * sin;

const mx = cx + (outerRadius + 30) * cos;

const my = cy + (outerRadius + 30) * sin;

const ex = mx + (cos >= 0 ? 1 : -1) * 22;

const ey = my;

const textAnchor = cos >= 0 ? 'start' : 'end';[1]


return (
  <g>
                <text    x={cx}    y={cy}    dy={8}
textAnchor="middle" fill={fill}>
        {payload.name}
    </text>
    <Sector
      cx={cx}
      cy={cy}
      innerRadius={innerRadius}
      outerRadius={outerRadius}
      startAngle={startAngle}
```

```
          endAngle={endAngle}

          fill={fill}

        />

        <Sector

          cx={cx}

          cy={cy}

          startAngle={startAngle}

          endAngle={endAngle}

          innerRadius={outerRadius + 6}

          outerRadius={outerRadius + 10}

          fill={fill}

        />

                                        <path
d={`M${sx},${sy}L${mx},${my}L${ex},${ey}`}
stroke={fill} fill="none" />

        <circle cx={ex} cy={ey} r={2} fill={fill}
stroke="none" />

        <text x={ex + (cos >= 0 ? 1 : -1) * 12}
y={ey} textAnchor={textAnchor} fill="#333">{`PV
${value}`}</text>

        <text x={ex + (cos >= 0 ? 1 : -1) * 12}
y={ey}      dy={18}      textAnchor={textAnchor}
fill="#999">
```

```
          {`(Rate ${(percent * 100).toFixed(2)}%)`}

        </text>[2]

      </g>

    );

};


function MyDoughnutChart() {

      const   [activeIndex,   setActiveIndex]   =
useState(0);

    const onPieEnter = (_, index) => {

      setActiveIndex(index);

    };


    return (

      <PieChart width={400} height={400}>[3]

        <Pie

          activeIndex={activeIndex}

          activeShape={renderActiveShape}

          data={data}

          cx={200}

          cy={200}
```

```
        innerRadius={60}

        outerRadius={80}

        fill="#8884d8"4

        dataKey="value"

        onMouseEnter={onPieEnter}

      />

    </PieChart>

  );

}



export default MyDoughnutChart;5
```

Explanation:

`activeShape`: This prop allows you to define a custom shape for the active (hovered) slice. The `renderActiveShape` function in the example creates a more visually appealing active slice with labels and a highlighted segment.

`activeIndex` and `onPieEnter`: These are used to track and handle the active slice.

These examples demonstrate how to create pie and doughnut charts with labels and customizations. You can further enhance them by adjusting colors, adding animations, and exploring other Recharts components and props to achieve the desired visual representation for your data.

Chapter 4

Advanced Charting Techniques

4.1 Interactive Charts (Tooltips, zooming, panning) - Code examples: adding tooltips to a line chart, implementing zoom and pan functionality

1. Adding Tooltips to a Line Chart

Tooltips provide details about data points when the user hovers over them. In Recharts, the `<Tooltip />` component makes this easy.

JavaScript

```javascript
import React from 'react';

import { LineChart, Line, XAxis, YAxis,
CartesianGrid, Tooltip, Legend } from 'recharts';


const data1 = [

  { date: '2024-11-20', value: 120 },

  // ... your data

];


function MyLineChart() {
```

```
    return (

        <LineChart  width={600}  height={300}
data={data}>

        {/* ... other components ... */}

        <Tooltip /> {/* Add the Tooltip component
*/}

        <Line  type="monotone"  dataKey="value"
stroke="#8884d8" />

    </LineChart>

  );

}


export default MyLineChart;
```

Customization: You can customize the tooltip's content, appearance, and behavior using props like:

`content`: Provide a custom React component to render the tooltip content.

`cursor`: Customize the cursor style on hover.

`wrapperStyle`: Apply custom styles to the tooltip wrapper.

`formatter`: Format the values displayed in the tooltip.

`labelFormatter`: Format the labels in the tooltip.

2. Implementing Zoom and Pan Functionality

Recharts doesn't have built-in zoom and pan features. However, you can achieve this using a combination of:

State Management: Store the zoom level and pan position in your component's state.

Event Handlers: Use event handlers (like onMouseDown, onMouseMove, onMouseUp) to track mouse interactions and update the state.

Transformations: Apply transformations (scaling and translating) to the chart elements based on the zoom and pan state.

Here's a simplified example demonstrating the basic concept (this will require more elaborate implementation for production use):

JavaScript

```javascript
import React, { useState } from 'react';

import { LineChart, Line, XAxis, YAxis,
CartesianGrid, Tooltip, Legend } from 'recharts';


const data2 = [ /* ... your data ... */ ];


function MyLineChart() {

  const [zoom, setZoom] = useState(1);

  const [panX, setPanX] = useState(0);


  const handleMouseDown = (e) => {
```

```javascript
    // ... logic to start panning (capture
initial mouse position)

  };



  const handleMouseMove = (e) => {

    // ... logic to update panX based on mouse
movement

    setPanX(/* ... calculate new panX ... */);

  };



  const handleMouseUp = (e) => {

   // ... logic to end panning

  };



  const handleWheel = (e) => {

    // ... logic to update zoom based on mouse
wheel

    setZoom(/* ... calculate new zoom ... */);

  };



  return (

    <LineChart
```

```jsx
      width={600}

      height={300}

      data={data}

      onMouseDown={handleMouseDown}

      onMouseMove={handleMouseMove}

      onMouseUp={handleMouseUp}

      onWheel={handleWheel}
    >

      {/* ... other components ... */}

      <Line

        type="monotone"

        dataKey="value"

        stroke="#8884d8"

            transform={`translate(${panX},  0)
scale(${zoom}, 1)`} // Apply transformations

      />

    </LineChart>

  );

}


export default MyLineChart;
```

Explanation:

We use state variables `zoom` and `panX` to keep track of the zoom level and horizontal pan position.

Event handlers (`handleMouseDown`, `handleMouseMove`, etc.) capture user interactions and update the state.

The `transform` attribute on the `<Line>` component applies the calculated transformations (translation for panning, scaling for zooming).

Important Notes:

This is a simplified example. A production-ready implementation would involve more complex logic for handling mouse events, boundary checks, and smooth transitions.

You might consider using a third-party library like `d3-zoom` or a custom React hook to handle zoom and pan behavior more effectively.

Recharts is primarily designed for creating static charts. If your primary focus is highly interactive charts with complex zoom and pan features, D3.js might be a more suitable choice.

4.2 Animations and Transitions (Making charts visually appealing) - Code examples: animating chart elements on data updates, transitions for smooth rendering

1. Animating Chart Elements on Data Updates

Recharts provides the `<Animated.>` wrapper components (e.g., `Animated.Line`, `Animated.Bar`, `Animated.Pie`) to add animations to your charts. These components animate changes in data, making the transitions visually smoother and more engaging.

Example: Animating a Line Chart

JavaScript

```javascript
import React from 'react';

import { LineChart, XAxis, YAxis, CartesianGrid, Tooltip, Legend, Animated } from 'recharts';


const data = [ /* ... your data ... */ ];


function MyLineChart() {

  return (

        <LineChart  width={600}  height={300} data={data}>

    {/* ... other components ... */}

    <Animated.Line

      type="monotone"

      dataKey="value"

      stroke="#8884d8"

        animationDuration={500} // Animation duration in milliseconds

    />
```

```
    </LineChart>

  );

}


export default MyLineChart;
```

Explanation:

We replace `<Line>` with `<Animated.Line>` to enable animations.

`animationDuration` controls how long the animation lasts.

When the data updates (e.g., when new data points are added or existing ones change), the line will animate smoothly to its new position.

Animation Types:

Recharts provides different animation easing functions (e.g., `easeIn`, `easeOut`, `easeInOut`) that you can apply to the `animationEasing` prop to control the animation's acceleration and deceleration.

2. Transitions for Smooth Rendering

Transitions are another way to create smooth visual effects in your charts. They can be used to animate the initial rendering of the chart or to smoothly transition between different chart states.

Example: Using `react-transition-group`

JavaScript

```jsx
import React, { useState } from 'react';

import { CSSTransition } from
'react-transition-group';

import { LineChart, Line, XAxis, YAxis,
CartesianGrid, Tooltip, Legend } from
'recharts';[1]


const data = [ /* ... your data ... */ ];


function MyLineChart() {
    const [showChart, setShowChart] =
useState(false);


  return (
    <div>
                    <button onClick={() =>
setShowChart(!showChart)}>
      {showChart ? 'Hide Chart' : 'Show Chart'}
    </button>


    <CSSTransition
      in={showChart}
      timeout={300}
```

```
        classNames="my-chart" // CSS class for
transitions

        unmountOnExit

    >

        <LineChart width={600} height={300}
data={data}>

        {/* ... chart components ... */}

        </LineChart>

    </CSSTransition>

  </div>

  );

}


export default MyLineChart;
```

Explanation:

We use `react-transition-group` to add transition effects.

`CSSTransition` wraps the `<LineChart>` component.

The `in` prop controls whether the chart is shown or hidden.

`timeout` specifies the transition duration.

`classNames` defines the CSS classes that will be applied during the transition. You'll need to define these classes in your CSS file to control the animation (e.g., fading in, sliding in).

3. Key Considerations

Performance: Be mindful of performance when using animations, especially with large datasets or complex animations.

Accessibility: Ensure that animations don't create accessibility issues (e.g., use appropriate ARIA attributes and avoid animations that may trigger seizures).

User Experience: Use animations thoughtfully to enhance the user experience, not distract from the data.

By using animations and transitions effectively, you can create dynamic and visually appealing charts that engage users and make your data visualizations more memorable.

4.3 Customizing Chart Appearance (Colors, fonts, legends) - Code examples: styling chart elements with CSS, creating custom legends

1. Styling with CSS

Recharts allows you to target specific chart elements using CSS classes. This gives you fine-grained control over the appearance of your charts.

Example: Styling a Line Chart

JavaScript

```
import React from 'react';

import { LineChart, Line, XAxis, YAxis,
CartesianGrid, Tooltip, Legend } from 'recharts';

import './MyLineChart.css'; // Import your CSS
file
```

```
const data = [ /* ... your data ... */ ];


function MyLineChart() {

  return (

          <LineChart   width={600}   height={300}
data={data} className="my-line-chart">

      <XAxis dataKey="name" className="my-x-axis"
/>

      <YAxis className="my-y-axis" />

              <CartesianGrid   stroke="#f5f5f5"
className="my-grid" />

      <Tooltip />

      <Legend />

          <Line  type="monotone"  dataKey="value"
stroke="#8884d8" className="my-line" />

    </LineChart>

  );

}


export default MyLineChart;
```

MyLineChart.css:

CSS

```css
.my-line-chart {

  font-family: 'Arial', sans-serif;

}


.my-x-axis .recharts-text {

  fill: #666;

  font-size: 12px;

}


.my-y-axis .recharts-text {

  fill: #666;

}


.my-grid line {

  stroke: #ccc;

}


.my-line {
```

```
  stroke-width: 2;
}
```

Explanation:

We add a `className` to the `<LineChart>` and its child components.

In the CSS file, we target these classes and their child elements (e.g., `.my-x-axis` `.recharts-text`) to apply styles.

You can customize colors, fonts, line styles, and more using standard CSS properties.

2. Creating Custom Legends

While Recharts provides a default `<Legend>` component, you might need more control over its appearance or behavior. Here's how to create a custom legend:

JavaScript

```javascript
import React from 'react';

import { LineChart, Line, XAxis, YAxis, CartesianGrid, Tooltip } from 'recharts';

const data = [ /* ... your data ... */ ];

const COLORS = ['#8884d8', '#82ca9d'];
```

```jsx
function MyLineChart() {

  return (

    <div>

          <LineChart  width={600}  height={300}
data={data}>

        {/* ... other components ... */}

        <Line type="monotone" dataKey="value1"
stroke={COLORS[0]} />

        <Line type="monotone" dataKey="value2"
stroke={COLORS[1]} />

      </LineChart>


      {/* Custom Legend */}

      <div className="my-legend">

        {data.map((entry, index) => (

                  <div  key={`item-${index}`}
className="legend-item">

              <div className="legend-color"
style={{ backgroundColor: COLORS[index] }}></div>

                              <span
className="legend-text">{entry.name}</span>

        </div>

      ))}
```

```
        </div>

      </div>

    );

}


export default MyLineChart;
```

Explanation:

We remove the default `<Legend>` component.

We create a custom legend using a `div` with the class `my-legend`.

Inside the `div`, we map over the data to create legend items with color boxes and labels.

You can style the legend using CSS to match your application's design.

3. Important Considerations:

Specificity: When using CSS, be mindful of CSS specificity rules to ensure your styles are applied correctly.

Recharts Structure: Familiarize yourself with the DOM structure that Recharts generates to effectively target elements with your CSS.

Accessibility: Make sure your custom styles and legends don't create accessibility issues. Use appropriate ARIA attributes and semantic HTML to maintain accessibility.

By combining CSS styling and custom components, you have great flexibility in customizing the appearance of your Recharts charts to create visually appealing and informative data visualizations.

Chapter 5

Data Handling and Management

5.1 Fetching Data from APIs (REST APIs, asynchronous requests) - Code examples: using fetch to retrieve data, handling loading states

1. Understanding REST APIs

REST (Representational State Transfer) APIs are a way for applications to communicate with each other over the internet. They use standard HTTP methods (GET, POST, PUT, DELETE) to interact with resources (data).

Endpoints: APIs expose endpoints (URLs) that represent specific resources or actions. For example, `https://api.example.com/users` might be an endpoint to retrieve a list of users.

JSON: Data is typically exchanged in JSON (JavaScript Object Notation) format, which is a lightweight and easy-to-parse data format.

2. Using `fetch` to Retrieve Data

The `fetch` API is a modern way to make asynchronous requests in JavaScript. It returns a Promise that resolves to the response from the server.

Example:

JavaScript

```javascript
import React, { useState, useEffect } from
'react';

import { LineChart, Line, XAxis, YAxis,
CartesianGrid, Tooltip, Legend } from
'recharts';[1]


function MyLineChart() {

  const [data,[2] setData] = useState([]);

      const [isLoading, setIsLoading] =
useState(true);


  useEffect(() => {

    const fetchData = async () => {

      try {

                const response = await
fetch('https://api.example.com/data');[3]        //
Replace with your API endpoint[4]

        const jsonData = await response.json();

        setData(jsonData);

      } catch (error) {

        console.error('Error fetching data:',
error);

      } finally {
```

```
        setIsLoading(false);

    }

  };



    fetchData();[5]

  }, []); // Empty dependency array ensures this
runs once on component mount



  if (isLoading) {

    return <div>Loading...</div>;

  }



  return (

        <LineChart   width={600}   height={300}
data={data}>

      {/* ... chart components ... */}

    </LineChart>

  );

}



export default MyLineChart;
```

Explanation:

We use `useState` to manage the chart data (`data`) and a loading state (`isLoading`).

`useEffect` is used to fetch the data when the component mounts.

Inside `useEffect`, we use `async/await` to handle the asynchronous `fetch` call.

We update the `data` state with the fetched data and set `isLoading` to `false` when the data is loaded or an error occurs.

We conditionally render a "Loading..." message while the data is being fetched.

3. Handling Loading States

It's important to provide feedback to the user while data is being loaded. Here are some common ways to handle loading states:

Loading Indicators: Display a loading spinner or progress bar.

Skeleton Screens: Show a placeholder UI that mimics the structure of the chart while the data loads.

Error Messages: Display an error message if the data fails to load, providing helpful information to the user.

4. Key Considerations

Error Handling: Implement robust error handling to gracefully handle network errors or API issues.

Data Transformation: You might need to transform the fetched data to match the format required by your charting library.

Caching: Consider caching the data to reduce the number of API calls and improve performance.

Authentication: If the API requires authentication, you'll need to include authentication headers in your `fetch` requests.

By following these practices, you can effectively fetch data from APIs and create dynamic, data-driven charts in your React applications.

5.2 Data Transformation and Preparation (Filtering, sorting, aggregation) - Code examples: using JavaScript array methods to prepare data for charts

You're spot on! Data transformation is often essential to get your data in the right shape for your charts. JavaScript provides powerful array methods that make this process efficient and clean. Let's explore some common scenarios:

1. Filtering Data

Use the `filter()` method to create a new array containing only the elements that meet a specific condition.

Example: Filtering data for a specific year

JavaScript

```javascript
const data = [

  { date: '2023-11-20', value: 120 },

  { date: '2024-11-21', value: 150 },

  { date: '2024-11-22', value: 130 },

  { date: '2023-11-23', value: 180 },

];
```

```
const    filteredData    =    data.filter(item    =>
item.date.startsWith('2024'));
```

```
// filteredData will be:

// [

//    { date: '2024-11-21', value: 150 },

//    { date: '2024-11-22', value: 130 }

// ]
```

2. Sorting Data

Use the `sort()` method to order the elements in an array based on a specified criterion.

Example: Sorting data by value in descending order

JavaScript

```
const data = [

  { category: 'A', value: 40 },

  { category: 'B', value: 70 },

  { category: 'C', value: 30 },

];
```

```javascript
const sortedData = data.sort((a, b) => b.value -
a.value);


// sortedData will be:

// [

//    { category: 'B', value: 70 },

//    { category: 'A', value: 40 },

//    { category: 'C', value: 30 }

// ]
```

3. Aggregation

Use the `reduce()` method to aggregate data, such as calculating sums, averages, or grouping data.

Example: Calculating the total value

JavaScript

```javascript
const data = [

  { category: 'A', value: 40 },

  { category: 'B', value: 70 },

  { category: 'C', value: 30 },

];
```

```javascript
const totalValue = data.reduce((sum, item) => sum
+ item.value, 0);


// totalValue will be 140
```

Example: Grouping data by category

JavaScript

```javascript
const data = [

  { category: 'A', value: 40 },

  { category: 'B', value: 70 },

  { category: 'A', value: 30 },

];


const groupedData = data.reduce((acc, item) => {

  const category = item.category;

  if (!acc[category]) {

    acc[category] = [];

  }

  acc[category].push(item);

  return acc;

}, {});
```

```javascript
// groupedData will be:

// {

//      A: [ { category: 'A', value: 40 }, {
category: 'A', value: 30 } ],

//   B: [ { category: 'B', value: 70 } ]

// }
```

4. Chaining Array Methods

You can chain these array methods to perform multiple
transformations in a concise way.

Example: Filtering, sorting, and then mapping

JavaScript

```javascript
const data = [ /* ... your data ... */ ];


const transformedData = data

   .filter(item => /* ... your filter condition
... */)

   .sort((a, b) => /* ... your sorting logic ...
*/)

  .map(item => ({

      // ... transform the item (e.g., extract
specific properties)
```

```
})) ;
```

5. Important Notes

Immutability: Array methods like `filter()`, `sort()`, and `map()` return new arrays without modifying the original array. This is important for maintaining data integrity and avoiding unexpected side effects.

Performance: For large datasets, consider performance implications when using these methods. You might need to optimize your transformations or use libraries that provide more efficient algorithms.

By mastering these JavaScript array methods, you can effectively transform and prepare your data for use in your Recharts charts, ensuring that your visualizations accurately and effectively represent the information you want to convey.

5.3 State Management for Chart Data (Updating charts dynamically) - Code examples: using React state to update chart data, handling user interactions

1. Why State Management is Important

Charts often need to respond to user interactions (filtering, selecting data points, etc.) or update with new data from APIs. React's state management capabilities are crucial for handling these dynamic updates. When the state changes, React re-renders the components, including your charts, to reflect the updated data.

2. Using React State to Update Chart Data

Here's an example of a bar chart that updates when the user clicks buttons to filter data:

JavaScript

```javascript
import React, { useState } from 'react';

import { BarChart, Bar, XAxis, YAxis, CartesianGrid, Tooltip, Legend } from 'recharts';


const initialData = [

  { category: 'A', value: 40, type: 'Electronics' },

  { category: 'B', value: 70, type: 'Clothing' },

  { category: 'C', value: 30, type: 'Books' },

  { category: 'D', value: 90, type: 'Electronics' },

  { category: 'E', value: 60, type: 'Clothing' },

];


function MyBarChart() {

  const [data, setData] = useState(initialData);


  const handleFilter = (type) => {
```

```jsx
  if (type === 'All') {

    setData(initialData);

  } else {

    const filteredData =
initialData.filter(item => item.type === type);

    setData(filteredData);

  }

};


  return (

    <div>

      <button onClick={() =>
handleFilter('All')}>All</button>
      <button onClick={() =>
handleFilter('Electronics')}>Electronics</button>
      <button onClick={() =>
handleFilter('Clothing')}>Clothing</button>


      <BarChart width={600} height={300}
data={data}>

        {/* ... chart components ... */}

      </BarChart>

    </div>
```

```
    );

}
```

```
export default MyBarChart;
```

Explanation:

We store the chart data in the `data` state variable, initialized with `initialData`.

The `handleFilter` function filters the data based on the selected category and updates the `data` state.

Clicking the buttons triggers `handleFilter`, causing the chart to re-render with the filtered data.

3. Handling User Interactions

Charts can be made more interactive by responding to user actions like clicks, hovers, or selections.

Example: Highlighting a bar on click

JavaScript

```
import React, { useState } from 'react';

import { BarChart, Bar, XAxis, YAxis,
CartesianGrid, Tooltip, Legend } from 'recharts';


const data = [ /* ... your data ... */ ];
```

```
function MyBarChart() {

    const [activeCategory, setActiveCategory] =
useState(null);


  const handleClick = (data, index) => {

    setActiveCategory(data.name);

  };


  return (

            <BarChart  width={600}  height={300}
data={data}>

      {/* ... other components ... */}

      <Bar

        dataKey="value"

        onClick={handleClick}

            fill={activeCategory === data.name ?
'#ff7300' : '#8884d8'}

      />

    </BarChart>

  );

}
```

```
export default MyBarChart;
```

Explanation:

We use `activeCategory` to track the currently selected category.

The `handleClick` function updates `activeCategory` with the clicked bar's category.

The `fill` color of the bars is conditionally set based on `activeCategory`.

4. Advanced State Management

For more complex applications, consider using a dedicated state management library like Redux, Zustand, or Recoil. These libraries provide:

Centralized State: Manage your application's state in a single store, making it easier to track and update.

Improved Performance: Optimize state updates and re-renders for better performance, especially with large datasets or complex interactions.

Debugging Tools: Provide tools for debugging and inspecting state changes.

By effectively managing your chart data with React state and potentially using a state management library, you can create dynamic and interactive data visualizations that respond to user actions and data updates seamlessly.

Chapter 6

Building Complex Charts

6.1 Stacked Charts and Grouped Charts (Visualizing multiple data series) - Code examples: creating stacked bar charts, grouped line charts

You're getting into some really useful chart types for comparing multiple data series! Here's how to create stacked bar charts and grouped line charts in Recharts:

1. Stacked Bar Charts

Stacked bar charts are great for showing the cumulative value of different categories over another variable (like time). Each bar is divided into segments representing the contribution of each category to the total.

Data Format:

JavaScript

```
const data = [

  { month: 'Jan', "Product A": 20, "Product B":
30, "Product C": 10 },

  { month: 'Feb', "Product A": 35, "Product B":
25, "Product C": 20 },

  { month: 'Mar', "Product A": 40, "Product B":
45, "Product C": 15 },
```

```
// ... more months
```

```
];
```

Code Example:

JavaScript

```javascript
import React from 'react';

import { BarChart, Bar, XAxis, YAxis, CartesianGrid, Tooltip, Legend } from 'recharts';


const data = [ /* ... your data as shown above ... */ ];


function MyStackedBarChart() {

  return (

        <BarChart width={600} height={300} data={data}>

    <XAxis dataKey="month" />

    <YAxis />

    <CartesianGrid strokeDasharray="3 3" />

    <Tooltip />

    <Legend />
```

```
            <Bar  dataKey="Product  A"  stackId="a"
fill="#8884d8" />

            <Bar  dataKey="Product  B"  stackId="a"
fill="#82ca9d" />

            <Bar  dataKey="Product  C"  stackId="a"
fill="#ffc658" />

    </BarChart>

  );

}


export default MyStackedBarChart;
```

Explanation:

We use multiple `<Bar>` components, each representing a data series ("Product A", "Product B", "Product C").

The `stackId="a"` prop is crucial. It tells Recharts to stack these bars on top of each other. If you want separate stacks, use different `stackId` values.

2. Grouped Line Charts

Grouped line charts are useful for comparing trends of multiple data series over time or another continuous variable.

Data Format: (Similar to stacked bar chart data)

JavaScript

```
const data = [
```

```javascript
  { month: 'Jan', "Series A": 120, "Series B": 80
},

  { month: 'Feb', "Series A": 150, "Series B":
110 },

  { month: 'Mar', "Series A": 130, "Series B": 95
},

  // ... more months

];
```

Code Example:

JavaScript

```javascript
import React from 'react';

import { LineChart, Line, XAxis, YAxis,
CartesianGrid, Tooltip, Legend } from 'recharts';


const data¹ = [ /* ... your data as shown above
... */ ];


function MyGroupedLineChart() {

  return (

          <LineChart  width={600}  height={300}
data={data}>

      <XAxis dataKey="month" />
```

```
    <YAxis />

    <CartesianGrid stroke="#f5f5f5" />

    <Tooltip />

    <Legend />

        <Line type="monotone" dataKey="Series A"
stroke="#8884d8" />

        <Line type="monotone" dataKey="Series B"
stroke="#82ca9d" />

    </LineChart>

  );

}


export default MyGroupedLineChart;
```

Explanation:

We use multiple `<Line>` components, each representing a data series ("Series A", "Series B").

Recharts automatically groups the lines based on the shared x-axis data ("month").

Important Notes:

Colors and Legends: Use distinct colors for each series and a clear legend to make the chart easy to understand.

Data Structure: Make sure your data is properly structured with consistent keys for the categories/series.

Chart Choice: Choose the chart type (stacked or grouped) that best represents the relationships in your data and the insights you want to highlight.

6.2 Area Charts and Scatter Plots (Visualizing trends and relationships) - Code examples: area chart with multiple series, interactive scatter plot

1. Area Charts with Multiple Series

Area charts are fantastic for visualizing trends over time and comparing the magnitudes of different categories. When you have multiple series, the areas stack on top of each other, showing the cumulative total.

Data Format:

JavaScript

```
const data = [

  { month: 'Jan', "Series A": 120, "Series B": 80
},

    { month: 'Feb', "Series A": 150, "Series B":
110 },

  { month: 'Mar', "Series A": 130, "Series B": 95
},

  // ... more months

];
```

Code Example:

JavaScript

```javascript
import React from 'react';

import { AreaChart, Area, XAxis, YAxis,
CartesianGrid, Tooltip, Legend } from 'recharts';


const data = [ /* ... your data as shown above
... */ ];


function MyAreaChart() {

  return (

        <AreaChart  width={600}  height={300}
data={data}>

    <XAxis dataKey="month" />

    <YAxis />

    <CartesianGrid stroke="#f5f5f5" />

    <Tooltip />

    <Legend />

      <Area type="monotone" dataKey="Series A"
stackId="1" stroke="#8884d8" fill="#8884d8" />

      <Area type="monotone" dataKey="Series B"
stackId="1" stroke="#82ca9d" fill="#82ca9d" />

    </AreaChart>
```

```
  );

}
```

```
export default MyAreaChart;
```

Explanation:

We use multiple `<Area>` components, each representing a data series.

`stackId="1"` ensures the areas are stacked. Use different `stackId` values for separate stacks.

`stroke` sets the color of the line, and `fill` sets the fill color of the area.

2. Interactive Scatter Plots

Scatter plots are ideal for visualizing the relationship between two variables. To make them interactive, we can add tooltips and potentially allow users to select data points.

Data Format:

JavaScript

```
const data = [

  { x: 10, y: 20, label: 'Point A' },

  { x: 30, y: 50, label: 'Point B' },

  { x: 20, y: 40, label: 'Point C' },

  // ... more points
```

```
];
```

Code Example:

JavaScript

```javascript
import React, { useState } from 'react';

import { ScatterChart, Scatter, XAxis, YAxis,
CartesianGrid, Tooltip, Legend } from 'recharts';


const data = [ /* ... your data as shown above
... */ ];


function MyScatterChart() {

    const [selectedPoint, setSelectedPoint] =
useState(null);


  const handleSelect = (data) => {

    setSelectedPoint(data);

  };


  return (

    <ScatterChart width={600} height={300}>

      <XAxis dataKey="x" />
```

```
    <YAxis dataKey="y" />

    <CartesianGrid />

     <Tooltip cursor={{ strokeDasharray: '3 3'
}} />

    <Legend />
    <Scatter
      name="My Scatter Plot"

      data={data}

      fill="#8884d8"

      onClick={handleSelect}

    >

      {data.map((entry, index) => (

       <Cell

         key={`cell-${index}`}

               fill={selectedPoint === entry ?
'#ff7300' : '#8884d8'}

       />

      ))}

    </Scatter>

  </ScatterChart>

  );
```

```
}
```

```
export default MyScatterChart;
```

Explanation:

We use `<ScatterChart>` and `<Scatter>` for the scatter plot.

`onClick={handleSelect}` allows users to click on data points.

`selectedPoint` state tracks the selected point.

We use `<Cell>` to conditionally change the color of the selected point.

Key Improvements:

Customization: Explore Recharts' customization options to style the chart elements (axes, grid, colors, etc.).

Tooltip Enhancement: Customize the tooltip content to display more information about each data point (e.g., `label`).

Advanced Interactions: Implement more complex interactions, like zooming, panning, or brushing, for deeper data exploration.

Accessibility: Ensure your interactive elements are accessible to users with disabilities.

By combining these techniques, you can create engaging and informative area charts and scatter plots that effectively visualize trends and relationships in your data.

6.3 Combining Chart Types (Creating hybrid visualizations) - Code examples: combining line and bar charts, creating custom chart layouts

You're thinking like a true data visualization pro! Combining chart types can lead to some really powerful and insightful displays. Here's how you can do it in Recharts:

1. Combining Line and Bar Charts

This combination is excellent for showing trends (line) alongside individual values (bars). Imagine showing monthly sales totals (bars) and a trend line of the average sale price (line).

Data Format:

JavaScript

```
const data = [

  { month: 'Jan', sales: 120, avgPrice: 25 },

  { month: 'Feb', sales: 150, avgPrice: 28 },

  { month: 'Mar', sales: 130, avgPrice: 26 },

  // ... more months

];
```

Code Example:

JavaScript

```
import React from 'react';
```

```jsx
import {

  ComposedChart,

  Line,

  Bar,

  XAxis,

  YAxis,

  CartesianGrid,

  Tooltip,

  Legend

} from 'recharts';


const data¹ = [ /* ... your data as shown above ... */ ];


function MyComboChart() {

  return (

      <ComposedChart width={600} height={300} data={data}>

      <XAxis dataKey="month" />

      <YAxis />

      <CartesianGrid stroke="#f5f5f5" />
```

```
    <Tooltip />

    <Legend />

            <Bar    dataKey="sales"    barSize={20}
fill="#413ea0" />

        <Line  type="monotone"  dataKey="avgPrice"
stroke="#ff7300" />

    </ComposedChart>

  );

}


export default MyComboChart;
```

Explanation:

We use `<ComposedChart>` to combine different chart types.

`<Bar>` displays the "sales" data as bars.

`<Line>` displays the "avgPrice" data as a line.

2. Creating Custom Chart Layouts

Recharts allows you to create more complex layouts by nesting charts or positioning them creatively.

Example: Line Chart with a Pie Chart Detail

JavaScript

```
import React from 'react';
```

```
import {

  LineChart,

  Line,

  XAxis,

  YAxis,

  CartesianGrid,

  Tooltip,

  PieChart,

  Pie

} from 'recharts';


const lineData = [ /* ... your line chart data
... */ ];

const pieData = [ /* ... your pie chart data ...
*/ ];


function MyCustomLayoutChart() {

  return (

    <div>

            <LineChart  width={600}  height={300}
data={lineData}>

        {/* ... line chart components ... */}
```

```
    </LineChart>


        <PieChart width={200} height={200> {/*
Position this as needed */}

            <Pie data={pieData} /* ... pie chart
components ... */ />

    </PieChart>

  </div>

  );

}


export default MyCustomLayoutChart;
```

Explanation:

We create a `<div>` to hold both charts.

We position the `<LineChart>` and `<PieChart>` within the `div`.

You can use CSS to control the exact layout and positioning of the charts.

Important Considerations:

Data Relationships: Make sure the combined chart types effectively represent the relationships in your data.

Visual Clarity: Maintain visual clarity and avoid overcrowding the chart.

Axes and Scales: If using multiple y-axes, ensure the scales are appropriate for each data series.

Responsiveness: Design your layout to be responsive to different screen sizes.

By creatively combining chart types and customizing layouts, you can create compelling hybrid visualizations that provide richer insights and tell more complete stories with your data.

Chapter 7

Responsive Charts and Accessibility

7.1 Making Charts Responsive (Adapting to different screen sizes) - Code examples: using CSS media queries to adjust chart size and layout

You're right to think about responsiveness! It's crucial for modern web applications. Here's how you can make your Recharts charts adapt to different screen sizes using CSS media queries:

1. Basic Responsive Chart

This example demonstrates a simple way to adjust the chart's width based on screen size.

JavaScript

```
import React from 'react';

import { LineChart, Line, XAxis, YAxis,
CartesianGrid, Tooltip, Legend } from 'recharts';

import './MyLineChart.css';


const data = [ /* ... your data ... */ ];


function MyLineChart() {
```

```
  return (

        <LineChart   width={600}   height={300}
data={data} className="responsive-chart">

    {/* ... chart components ... */}

  </LineChart>

  );

}


export default MyLineChart;
```

MyLineChart.css:

CSS

```
.responsive-chart {

  width: 100%; /* Chart takes full width of its
container */

  max-width: 600px; /* But doesn't exceed 600px
*/

}


@media (max-width: 500px) {

  .responsive-chart {
```

```
    height: 200px; /* Adjust height on smaller
screens */


  }

}
```

Explanation:

We set the chart's `width` to `100%` so it fills its container.

`max-width: 600px` prevents the chart from becoming too wide on large screens.

The media query `@media (max-width: 500px)` applies styles when the screen width is 500px or less. In this case, we reduce the chart's height.

2. Adjusting Layout with Media Queries

For more complex layouts, you can use media queries to rearrange chart elements.

CSS

```
@media (max-width: 768px) {

    .my-chart-container { /* Container holding
multiple charts */

        flex-direction: column; /* Stack charts
vertically */

    }


    .responsive-chart {
```

```
    margin-bottom: 20px; /* Add spacing between
stacked charts */

  }

}
```

Explanation:

This media query targets screens with a maximum width of 768px (typical for tablets).

It changes the `flex-direction` of the `.my-chart-container` (assuming you're using Flexbox) to stack the charts vertically.

It adds a `margin-bottom` to the `.responsive-chart` to create space between the charts.

3. Advanced Techniques

Responsive Container: Recharts provides a `<ResponsiveContainer>` component that can automatically adjust the chart's size to fit its parent container. This can be useful in some cases, but you might still need media queries for more fine-grained control.

Dynamic Data: Consider adjusting the amount of data displayed based on screen size. On smaller screens, you might show a simplified version of the chart or aggregate data to avoid overcrowding.

Orientation: Use media queries to adjust the layout based on screen orientation (portrait or landscape).

Key Considerations:

Breakpoints: Choose appropriate breakpoints for your media queries based on the design of your application and the devices you want to support.

Testing: Test your responsive charts on different devices and screen sizes to ensure they look good and function correctly.

Accessibility: Maintain accessibility as you adjust the layout. Ensure that interactive elements remain usable and that the chart is still readable on smaller screens.

By using CSS media queries effectively, you can create responsive Recharts charts that adapt seamlessly to different screen sizes, providing an optimal viewing experience for all users.

7.2 Accessibility Considerations (ARIA attributes, keyboard navigation) - Code examples: adding ARIA labels to chart elements, ensuring keyboard accessibility

Accessibility is essential to ensure that everyone, including people with disabilities, can perceive, understand, and interact with your charts. Here's how to improve the accessibility of your Recharts charts using ARIA attributes and keyboard navigation:

1. ARIA Attributes

ARIA (Accessible Rich Internet Applications) attributes provide semantic information to assistive technologies like screen readers.

`aria-label` **and** `aria-labelledby`: These attributes provide labels for elements that don't have visible labels.

JavaScript

```
<LineChart width={600} height={300} data={data}
aria-label="Monthly sales trend">

    {/* ... chart components ... */}

</LineChart>
```

In this example, `aria-label` provides a descriptive label for the chart.

`aria-describedby`: This attribute associates an element with another element that provides a more detailed description.

JavaScript

```
<LineChart

    width={600}

    height={300}

    data={data}

    aria-labelledby="chart-title"

    aria-describedby="chart-description"

>

    {/* ... chart components ... */}

</LineChart>


<h2 id="chart-title">Monthly Sales Trend</h2>
```

```
<p    id="chart-description">This    line    chart
displays  the  monthly  sales  figures  for  the  past
year.</p>
```

`aria-labelledby` links the chart to the `<h2>` heading for the title.

`aria-describedby` links the chart to the `<p>` element for a longer description.

Roles: Use ARIA roles (e.g., `role="img"`, `role="button"`) to define the semantic purpose of elements.

2. Keyboard Navigation

Ensure users can navigate and interact with your charts using the keyboard.

Focusable Elements: Make interactive chart elements (e.g., legend items, data points with tooltips) focusable using the `tabIndex="0"` attribute.

JavaScript

```
<Legend

  onClick={handleClick}

  onKeyPress={handleKeyPress}

  tabIndex="0"

/>
```

Keyboard Events: Handle keyboard events (e.g., `onKeyPress`, `onKeyDown`) to provide keyboard-based interactions.

JavaScript

```
const handleKeyPress = (event) => {

  if (event.key === 'Enter') {

      // Perform the same action as the onClick
handler

    handleClick();

  }

};
```

Visual Focus Indicators: Provide clear visual indicators when elements are focused using CSS (e.g., outline, box-shadow).

3. Other Considerations

Color Contrast: Ensure sufficient color contrast between chart elements and the background for people with low vision.

Alternative Text: Provide alternative text descriptions for charts that convey the key information for users who cannot see the visual representation. You can use the `<figcaption>` element or the `aria-describedby` attribute to associate the description with the chart.

Interactive Elements: If you have interactive elements (e.g., zoom, pan, filters), ensure they are keyboard accessible and provide clear instructions for users.

Example: Accessible Tooltip

JavaScript

```javascript
import React from 'react';

import { LineChart, Line, XAxis, YAxis, CartesianGrid, Tooltip, Legend } from 'recharts';


function MyLineChart()[1] {

  return (

          <LineChart  width={600}  height={300} data={data} aria-label="Sales trend">

      {/* ... other components ... */}

      <Tooltip

        content={<CustomTooltip />}

        cursor={{ strokeDasharray: '3 3' }}

          tabIndex="0"  // Make the tooltip focusable

      />

          <Line type="monotone" dataKey="sales" stroke="#8884d8" />

      </LineChart>
```

```jsx
  );

}


const CustomTooltip = ({ active, payload, label
}) => {

  if (active && payload && payload.length) {

    return (

            <div   className="custom-tooltip"[2]
role="tooltip" aria-label={`Sales for ${label}:
${payload[0].value}`}>

      {/* ARIA label for screen readers */}

            <p className="label">{`${label}  :
${payload[0].value}`}</p>

      </div>

    );

  }



  return null;

};



export default MyLineChart;
```

By incorporating ARIA attributes, keyboard navigation, and other accessibility best practices, you can create Recharts charts that are inclusive and usable for everyone.

7.3Optimizing Chart Performance (Lazy loading, code splitting) - Code examples: techniques for improving chart rendering performance

Optimizing chart performance is key to ensuring a smooth and responsive user experience, especially when dealing with complex charts or large datasets. Here are some techniques you can use to improve the rendering performance of your Recharts charts:

1. Lazy Loading

Lazy loading allows you to defer the loading of non-critical components until they are needed. This can significantly reduce the initial load time of your application.

`React.lazy()` **and** `Suspense`:

JavaScript

```javascript
import React, { lazy, Suspense } from 'react';


const MyLineChart = lazy(() => import('./MyLineChart')); // Lazy load the chart component


function App() {
```

```
return (
    <div>
            <Suspense    fallback={<div>Loading
Chart...</div>}>
        <MyLineChart />
      </Suspense>
    </div>
  );
}
```

Explanation:

`React.lazy()` allows you to dynamically import a component.

`Suspense` provides a fallback UI (e.g., a loading indicator) while the component is being loaded.

2. Code Splitting

Code splitting breaks your JavaScript bundle into smaller chunks, allowing the browser to load only the necessary code for the initial render.

Dynamic Imports:

JavaScript

```
import React, { useState, useEffect } from
'react';
```

```
function MyChartContainer() {

    const [ChartComponent, setChartComponent] =
useState(null);


  useEffect(() => {

    const fetchChartComponent = async () => {

        const { default: Component } = await
import('./MyLineChart');

      setChartComponent(() => Component);

    };


    fetchChartComponent();

  }, []);


  if (!ChartComponent) {

    return <div>Loading Chart...</div>;

  }


  return <ChartComponent />;

}
```

Explanation:

We dynamically import the `MyLineChart` component when the `MyChartContainer` mounts.

This creates a separate chunk for the chart component, which is loaded on demand.

3. Data Optimization

Data Filtering and Aggregation: Pre-process your data to reduce the amount of data that needs to be rendered. Filter out unnecessary data points or aggregate data to reduce the number of elements in the chart.

Data Structures: Use efficient data structures that are optimized for the type of chart you are creating. For example, if you have time-series data, consider using a library like `moment` or `date-fns` to efficiently handle date operations.

4. Recharts-Specific Optimizations

Avoid Unnecessary Re-renders: Use memoization techniques like `React.memo()` or `useMemo()` to prevent unnecessary re-renders of your chart components.

Limit Animations: Animations can be expensive, especially with large datasets. Use them sparingly and consider disabling animations on less powerful devices.

Windowing: For very large datasets, consider using windowing techniques to render only the visible portion of the chart. Recharts doesn't have built-in windowing, but you can implement it yourself or use a third-party library.

5. General Performance Tips

Profiling: Use browser profiling tools to identify performance bottlenecks in your chart rendering.

Code Optimization: Optimize your JavaScript code to reduce unnecessary calculations and DOM manipulations.

Caching: Cache data and chart components where possible to avoid redundant computations.

By implementing these optimization techniques, you can significantly improve the performance of your Recharts charts, resulting in a smoother and more responsive user experience.

Chapter 8

Real-World Charting Applications

8.1 Building a Dashboard with Multiple Charts (Integrating charts into a user interface) - Code examples: creating a dashboard layout, connecting charts to data sources

1. Planning the Layout

Before you start coding, think about how you want to arrange your charts on the dashboard. Consider:

Grid System: Use a CSS grid system (like Grid or Flexbox) to create a flexible and responsive layout.

Chart Relationships: Group related charts together to improve readability and information flow.

Information Hierarchy: Position the most important charts prominently.

Whitespace: Use whitespace effectively to avoid overcrowding and improve visual clarity.

2. Creating the Dashboard Layout

Here's an example of a dashboard layout using a CSS grid:

JavaScript

```
import React from 'react';

import MyLineChart from './MyLineChart';

import MyBarChart from './MyBarChart';
```

```jsx
import MyPieChart from './MyPieChart';

import './Dashboard.css';


function Dashboard() {
  return (
    <div className="dashboard">
      <div className="chart-grid">
        <div className="chart-item">
          <MyLineChart />
        </div>
        <div className="chart-item">
          <MyBarChart />
        </div>
        <div className="chart-item">
          <MyPieChart />
        </div>
      </div>
    </div>
  );
}
```

```
export default Dashboard;
```

Dashboard.css:

CSS

```css
.dashboard {

  padding: 20px;

}


.chart-grid {

  display: grid;

      grid-template-columns:    repeat(auto-fit,
minmax(300px, 1fr)); /* Responsive columns */

  grid-gap: 20px;

}


.chart-item {

  border: 1px solid #ccc;

  padding: 10px;

}
```

Explanation:

We create a `dashboard` container.

Inside, we use `chart-grid` with `grid-template-columns` to create responsive columns that adjust based on screen size.

Each `chart-item` holds an individual chart component.

3. Connecting Charts to Data Sources

You have a few options for connecting your charts to data sources:

Props: Pass data directly to the chart components as props. This works well for simple dashboards or when you have static data.

JavaScript

```
<MyLineChart data={lineChartData} />
```

State Management: Use a state management library (like Redux, Zustand, or Context API) to store and share data between components. This is ideal for more complex dashboards with dynamic data and interactions.

JavaScript

```
// In your chart component:

const    lineChartData    =    useSelector(state    =>
state.chartData.lineData);
```

```
<MyLineChart data={lineChartData} />
```

API Calls: Fetch data from APIs directly within your chart components (as shown in previous examples) or in a parent component that manages the data for the dashboard.

4. Key Considerations

Performance: Optimize data fetching and rendering to avoid performance issues with multiple charts.

Consistency: Maintain a consistent design and style across all charts on the dashboard.

Interactivity: Consider adding interactive elements (filters, tooltips, drill-downs) to enhance the dashboard's functionality.

Accessibility: Ensure the dashboard is accessible to users with disabilities by following accessibility best practices.

By following these steps, you can effectively build dashboards with multiple Recharts charts, creating a powerful and informative data visualization experience for your users.

8.2 Creating a Data Exploration Tool (Interactive filtering, drill-down) - Code examples: implementing filtering and drill-down functionality for data exploration

1. Data Structure for Drill-Down

To enable drill-down, you'll need hierarchical data. Here's an example of sales data organized by region, then by city:

JavaScript

```javascript
const data = [

  {

    region: 'North',

    sales: 1500,

    cities: [

      { city: 'City A', sales: 500 },

      { city: 'City B', sales: 600 },

      { city: 'City C', sales: 400 },

    ],

  },

  {

    region: 'South',

    sales: 1200,

    cities: [

      { city: 'City D', sales: 700 },

      { city: 'City E', sales: 500 },

    ],

  },

  // ... more regions
```

```javascript
];
```

2. Implementing Interactive Filtering

Let's create a bar chart that allows filtering by region:

JavaScript

```javascript
import React, { useState } from 'react';

import { BarChart, Bar, XAxis, YAxis,
CartesianGrid, Tooltip, Legend } from 'recharts';


const data = [ /* ... your data as shown above
... */ ];


function MyBarChart() {

    const [selectedRegion, setSelectedRegion] =
useState(null);


  const handleFilter = (region) => {

    setSelectedRegion(region);

  };


  const filteredData = selectedRegion
```

```jsx
      ? data.filter((item) => item.region ===
selectedRegion)

    : data;


  return (

    <div>

      <div>

        {data.map((item) => (

            <button key={item.region} onClick={()
=> handleFilter(item.region)}>

            {item.region}

          </button>

        ))}

                    <button onClick={() =>
handleFilter(null)}>All Regions</button>

      </div>



          <BarChart width={600} height={300}
data={filteredData}>

        {/* ... chart components ... */}

        <Bar dataKey="sales" fill="#8884d8" />

        </BarChart>
```

```
      </div>

  );

}



export default MyBarChart;
```

Explanation:

`selectedRegion` state tracks the selected region.

`handleFilter` updates the `selectedRegion`.

`filteredData` is calculated based on the `selectedRegion`.

The chart re-renders with the `filteredData`.

3. Implementing Drill-Down

Now, let's add drill-down functionality to the bar chart:

JavaScript

```
import React, { useState } from 'react';

import { BarChart, Bar, XAxis, YAxis,
CartesianGrid, Tooltip, Legend } from 'recharts';



const data = [ /* ... your data as shown above
... */ ];



function MyBarChart() {
```

```
  const [selectedRegion, setSelectedRegion] =
useState(null);

  const [drillDownData, setDrillDownData] =
useState(null);


const handleFilter = (region) => {

  setSelectedRegion(region);

  setDrillDownData(null); // Reset drill-down
when filtering

  };


const handleDrillDown = (region) => {

    const regionData = data.find((item) =>
item.region === region);

          setDrillDownData(regionData ?
regionData.cities : null);

  };


const chartData = drillDownData ? drillDownData
: data;

  const dataKey = drillDownData ? 'sales' :
'sales'; // Use 'sales' for both levels

  const xAxisDataKey = drillDownData ? 'city' :
'region';
```

```jsx
  return (

    <div>

      {/* ... filtering buttons ... */}


            <BarChart  width={600}  height={300}
data={chartData}>

        {/* ... chart components ... */}

        <XAxis dataKey={xAxisDataKey} />

            <Bar  dataKey={dataKey}  fill="#8884d8"
onClick={(data) => handleDrillDown(data.name)} />

      </BarChart>


      {drillDownData && (

                    <button   onClick={()    =>
setDrillDownData(null)}>Go Back</button>

      )}

    </div>

  );

}


export default MyBarChart;
```

Explanation:

`drillDownData` state stores the data for the drilled-down level.

`handleDrillDown` finds the cities for the clicked region and updates `drillDownData`.

`chartData`, `dataKey`, and `xAxisDataKey` are dynamically determined based on the drill-down state.

Clicking a bar drills down to the city level.

A "Go Back" button allows the user to return to the region level.

Key Improvements:

Visual Cues: Provide visual cues (e.g., different colors, highlighting) to indicate interactive elements and the current drill-down level.

Animations: Use animations to make the transitions between levels smoother.

Data Loading: For large datasets, consider loading drill-down data on demand to improve initial load time.

Accessibility: Ensure the filtering and drill-down interactions are accessible via keyboard.

By combining interactive filtering and drill-down functionality, you can create powerful data exploration tools that allow users to analyze data at different levels of granularity and uncover valuable insights.

8.3 Visualizing Real-Time Data (WebSockets, data streaming) - Code examples: using WebSockets to update charts with real-time data

1. Understanding WebSockets

WebSockets provide a way to establish a persistent, bidirectional connection between a client (your web application) and a server. This allows for real-time communication, where the server can push data to the client as soon as it becomes available, without the client needing to constantly poll the server.

2. Setting up a WebSocket Connection

JavaScript

```
import React, { useState, useEffect } from 'react';

import { LineChart, Line, XAxis, YAxis, CartesianGrid, Tooltip, Legend } from 'recharts';[1]


const ws = new WebSocket('wss://your-websocket-server'); // Replace with your WebSocket server URL


function MyRealTimeChart() {

  const [data, setData] = useState([]);
```

```javascript
useEffect(() => {

  ws.onopen = () => {

    console.log('WebSocket connection opened');

  };


  ws.onmessage = (event) => {

                    const    newDataPoint    =
JSON.parse(event.data);

         setData((prevData)  =>  [...prevData,
newDataPoint]);

  };


  ws.onclose = () => {

    console.log('WebSocket connection closed');

  };


  return () => {

      ws.close(); // Close the connection when
the component unmounts

  };

}, []);
```

```jsx
  return (

          <LineChart    width={600}    height={300}
data={data}>

      {/* ... chart components ... */}

    </LineChart>

  );

}


export default MyRealTimeChart;
```

Explanation:

We create a new `WebSocket` object, providing the URL of your WebSocket server.

In the `useEffect` hook:

`ws.onopen`: Handles the connection opening.

`ws.onmessage`: Handles incoming messages from the server. We parse the data (assuming it's in JSON format) and update the `data` state using a callback to preserve previous data points.

`ws.onclose`: Handles the connection closing.

The cleanup function closes the connection when the component unmounts.

3. Server-Side Implementation

You'll need a server-side component (e.g., using Node.js with a library like ws or socket.io) to handle the WebSocket connections and send data to the clients. This is a basic example using the ws library:

JavaScript

```javascript
const WebSocket = require('ws');


const wss = new WebSocket.Server({ port: 8080 });


wss.on('connection',² function connection(ws) {

  ws.on('message', function incoming(message) {

    console.log('received: %s', message);

  });


  // Simulate³ sending data every 2 seconds

  setInterval(() => {

    const newData = {

      time: new Date().toLocaleTimeString(),

      value: Math.random() * 100,

    };

    ws.send(JSON.stringify(newData));
```

```
    }, 2000);

});
```

4. Important Considerations

Data Handling: Handle incoming data efficiently. You might need to limit the number of data points stored in the `data` state to prevent performance issues.

Error Handling: Implement error handling for WebSocket events (e.g., connection errors, data parsing errors).

Connection Management: Handle connection closures and reconnections gracefully.

Security: Secure your WebSocket connection if you're transmitting sensitive data.

Key Improvements:

Data Sampling: If the data stream is very high-frequency, consider sampling the data on the client-side to reduce the rendering load.

Chart Optimization: Use the optimization techniques mentioned earlier (lazy loading, code splitting, memoization) to improve chart performance.

User Experience: Provide visual feedback to the user about the connection status (connected, disconnected, reconnecting).

By implementing WebSockets and these best practices, you can create dynamic charts that update in real-time, providing users with up-to-the-minute information and a more engaging experience.

Chapter 9

Testing and Debugging

9.1 Unit Testing Chart Components (Jest, React Testing Library) - Code examples: writing unit tests for chart components, testing data handling logic

1. Setting up the Testing Environment

Install Jest and React Testing Library:

Bash

```bash
npm install --save-dev jest @testing-library/react @testing-library/jest-dom
```

Create a Test File: Create a file named `MyLineChart.test.js` (or similar) alongside your chart component file (`MyLineChart.js`).

2. Writing Unit Tests

Here's an example of how to write unit tests for a simple line chart component:

JavaScript

```javascript
import React from 'react';

import { render, screen } from '@testing-library/react';
```

```
import { LineChart, Line, XAxis, YAxis } from
'recharts';

import MyLineChart from './MyLineChart';


const data = [

  { name: 'Page A', uv: 4000 },

  { name: 'Page B', uv: 3000 },

];


describe('MyLineChart', () => {

  it('renders the chart with the correct data',
() => {

    render(<MyLineChart data={data} />);


    // Check if the chart elements are present


expect(screen.getByRole('figure')).toBeInTheDocum
ent(); // The chart itself

                expect(screen.getByText('Page
A')).toBeInTheDocument(); // X-axis label

                expect(screen.getByText('Page
B')).toBeInTheDocument(); // X-axis label

  });
```

```
it('updates the chart when the data changes',
() => {

    const { rerender } = render(<MyLineChart
data={data} />);



    // Update the data

    const newData = [

      { name: 'Page C', uv: 5000 },

      { name: 'Page D', uv: 2000 },

    ];

    rerender(<MyLineChart data={newData} />);



    // Check if the chart reflects the new data

            expect(screen.getByText('Page
C')).toBeInTheDocument();

            expect(screen.getByText('Page
D')).toBeInTheDocument();

  });

});
```

Explanation:

We use `render` from React Testing Library to render the `MyLineChart` component.

`screen` provides utilities to query the rendered component.

We use `expect` and assertions from Jest to verify the expected behavior.

In the first test, we check if the chart and some basic labels are rendered.

In the second test, we use `rerender` to update the chart with new data and check if the chart updates accordingly.

3. Testing Data Handling Logic

You can also test the internal data handling logic of your chart components.

JavaScript

```javascript
import React from 'react';

import { render, screen } from '@testing-library/react';

import MyLineChart from './MyLineChart';


describe('MyLineChart', () => {

  it('formats the data correctly', () => {

    const rawData = [

      { date: '2024-11-28', value: 120 },

      // ... more data
```

```
    ];

    render(<MyLineChart data={rawData} />);


    // Assuming MyLineChart formats dates to 'Nov
28'

                      expect(screen.getByText('Nov
28')).toBeInTheDocument();

  });

});
```

Explanation:

We provide raw data to the chart component.

We then check if the chart displays the data in the expected formatted way (e.g., 'Nov 28' instead of '2024-11-28').

4. Key Considerations

Focus on User Interactions: Test how the chart behaves from the user's perspective.

Test Edge Cases: Test with different data scenarios, including empty datasets, edge values, and invalid data.

Mock External Dependencies: If your chart component interacts with external APIs or services, mock those dependencies to isolate the component's logic.

Code Coverage: Use Jest's code coverage reporting to track how much of your code is covered by tests.

By writing comprehensive unit tests for your Recharts components, you can ensure that your charts are rendering correctly, handling data as expected, and providing a reliable and consistent user experience.

9.2 Debugging Chart Issues (Browser developer tools, common problems)

Debugging is an essential skill for any developer, and when it comes to charts, the browser developer tools are your best friend. Here's how you can use them effectively to troubleshoot common chart issues in Recharts:

1. Browser Developer Tools

Console: The console is your primary source of information for errors, warnings, and logging messages. Use `console.log` to inspect variables, data, and component props within your chart code.

Elements Tab: Inspect the HTML structure of your chart. Recharts generates SVG elements, so understanding the structure can help you identify rendering issues or apply CSS styles more effectively.

Network Tab: Monitor network requests related to your chart data. This is crucial if you're fetching data from APIs. Check for errors, loading times, and data formats.

Performance Tab: Analyze the performance of your chart rendering. Identify potential bottlenecks and optimize your code for smoother interactions.

2. Common Chart Issues and Debugging Techniques

Data Issues:

Incorrect Format: Verify that your data is in the format expected by Recharts (usually an array of objects with the correct `dataKey` properties). Use `console.log` to inspect the data before it's passed to the chart component.

Missing Data: Check if your data is being fetched correctly from APIs. Use the Network tab to monitor API requests and responses.

Data Transformation Errors: If you're transforming data before passing it to the chart, use `console.log` to check the output of your transformations at each step.

Rendering Issues:

No Chart Displayed: Check the console for errors. Inspect the Elements tab to see if the chart elements are being rendered at all. Verify that you're providing the correct `width` and `height` props to the chart component.

Incorrect Chart Type: Ensure you're using the correct chart component (e.g., `LineChart`, `BarChart`, `PieChart`) for the type of visualization you want.

Styling Problems: Use the Elements tab to inspect the CSS styles applied to the chart elements. Check for conflicting styles or incorrect class names.

Interaction Issues:

Tooltips Not Working: Verify that you've included the `<Tooltip />` component within your chart. Use `console.log` to check if the `payload` and `label` props are being passed correctly to the tooltip content.

Zooming/Panning Not Smooth: If you've implemented custom zooming or panning, use the Performance tab to profile the code and identify potential performance bottlenecks.

Performance Issues:

Slow Rendering: Use the Performance tab to analyze the rendering time of your chart. Identify long-running tasks and optimize your code using techniques like lazy loading, code splitting, and memoization.

High CPU Usage: Monitor CPU usage in the Performance tab. If your chart is causing high CPU usage, consider reducing the complexity of the chart, limiting animations, or optimizing data handling.

3. Debugging Tips

Start Simple: If you're facing issues, try creating a minimal reproducible example with a simple chart and data. This can help isolate the problem.

Read the Documentation: The Recharts documentation is a valuable resource for understanding the library's API, common issues, and troubleshooting tips.

Use `console.log` **Extensively:** Don't hesitate to use `console.log` to inspect variables, data, and component props at various points in your code.

Breakpoints: Use breakpoints in the Sources tab of the developer tools to pause code execution and step through your code line by line.

By effectively utilizing the browser developer tools and following these debugging techniques, you can quickly identify and resolve issues in your Recharts charts, ensuring that your data visualizations are accurate, performant, and provide a great user experience.

9.3 Performance Profiling and Optimization (Identifying and addressing performance bottlenecks)

Performance profiling and optimization are crucial for ensuring your Recharts visualizations run smoothly, especially with complex charts or large datasets. Here's a breakdown of the process:

1. Identifying Performance Bottlenecks

Chrome DevTools Performance Profiler:

Record a performance profile while interacting with your chart.

Analyze the Flame Chart to identify functions or events taking the most time.

Look for long "bars" in the Flame Chart, which indicate functions with high execution time.

Pay attention to "red" bars, which might indicate performance issues.

React Profiler:

Use the React Profiler (available in React DevTools) to measure the render performance of your React components.

Identify components that re-render frequently or take a long time to render.

User Timing API:

Use the `performance.mark()` and `performance.measure()` methods to measure specific code blocks in your chart components.

This can help you pinpoint performance bottlenecks in your data processing or rendering logic.

2. Addressing Performance Bottlenecks

Data Optimization:

Reduce Data Size: Filter or aggregate data to reduce the number of data points rendered.

Optimize Data Structures: Use efficient data structures for your data (e.g., arrays, maps).

Lazy Load Data: Load large datasets in chunks or on demand.

Component Optimization:

Memoization: Use `React.memo()`, `useMemo()`, or `useCallback()` to prevent unnecessary re-renders.

Code Splitting: Split your code into smaller chunks to reduce initial load time.

Lazy Loading: Lazy load non-critical chart components.

Rendering Optimization:

Windowing: Render only the visible portion of the chart for large datasets (Recharts doesn't have built-in windowing, so you'll need to implement it yourself or use a library).

Debouncing/Throttling: Limit the rate of updates for interactive charts (e.g., debounce resize events).

Reduce Animations: Use animations sparingly, as they can be expensive.

Recharts-Specific Optimizations:

Child Components: Only include necessary child components (e.g., `<Tooltip>`, `<Legend>`) within your chart.

Avoid Unnecessary Updates: Prevent unnecessary state updates that trigger re-renders.

3. Example: Optimizing a Line Chart

Let's say your line chart is slow to render due to a large dataset and frequent updates:

JavaScript

```javascript
import React, { useState, useEffect, useMemo } from 'react';

import { LineChart, Line, XAxis, YAxis } from 'recharts';


function MyLineChart({ data }) {

    const [filteredData, setFilteredData] = useState(data);


  // ... filtering logic ...


    // Memoize the filtered data to prevent unnecessary re-renders
  const memoizedData = useMemo(() => {

    // ... data filtering logic ...

    return filteredData;

    }, [filteredData]); // Only re-compute when filteredData changes
```

```
    return (

        <LineChart    width={600}    height={300}
data={memoizedData}>

      {/* ... chart components ... */}

    </LineChart>

  );

}
```

Explanation:

We use `useMemo()` to memoize the `filteredData` so that the chart doesn't re-render unnecessarily when other parts of the component update.

This optimization can significantly improve performance, especially if the filtering logic is complex or the data is large.

Key Takeaways:

Profiling is Essential: Use profiling tools to identify performance bottlenecks before making optimizations.

Focus on the Biggest Issues: Address the most significant performance issues first.

Test and Measure: After making optimizations, test and measure the performance to ensure the changes are effective.

Balance Performance with Features: Find a balance between performance and the features and complexity of your charts.

By systematically profiling, identifying bottlenecks, and applying optimization techniques, you can ensure your Recharts visualizations are performant, responsive, and provide a great user experience.

Chapter 10

Beyond the Basics

10.1 Exploring Advanced Libraries (D3.js for custom visualizations) - Code examples: basic D3.js integration, creating custom chart elements

While Recharts is excellent for common chart types, sometimes you need the ultimate flexibility and control that D3.js provides. Here's how to integrate D3.js into your React projects for custom visualizations:

1. Installation

Install D3.js using npm or yarn:

Bash

```
npm install d3
```

2. Basic D3.js Integration

Here's an example of creating a simple bar chart using D3.js within a React component:

JavaScript

```
import React, { useRef, useEffect } from 'react';

import * as d3 from 'd3';
```

```
const data = [
  { label: 'A', value: 10 },
  { label: 'B', value: 20 },
  { label: 'C', value: 15 },
];


function MyD3BarChart() {
  const svgRef = useRef();


  useEffect(() => {
    const svg = d3.select(svgRef.current);
    const width = 600;
    const height = 300;
    const margin = { top: 20, right: 20, bottom: 30, left: 40 };


    const x = d3
      .scaleBand()
      .domain(data.map((d) => d.label))
      .range([margin.left, width - margin.right])
```

```
  .padding(0.1);


const y = d3

  .scaleLinear()

  .domain([0, d3.max(data, (d) => d.value)])[1]

        .range([height  -  margin.bottom,
margin.top]);[2]


svg

  .selectAll('.bar')

  .data(data)

  .join('rect')

  .attr('class', 'bar')

  .attr('x', (d) => x(d.label))

  .attr('y', (d) => y(d.value))

  .attr('width', x.bandwidth())

  .attr('height', (d) => y(0) - y(d.value))

  .attr('fill',[3] 'steelblue');


svg

  .append('g')
```

```
        .attr('transform', `translate(0,${height -
margin.bottom})`)

        .call(d3.axisBottom(x));



    svg

      .append('g')

                            .attr('transform',[4]
`translate(${margin.left},0)`)

      .call(d3.axisLeft(y));

  }, [data]); // Re-render[5] if data changes



  return (

              <svg    ref={svgRef}    width={600}
height={300}></svg>

  );

}



export default MyD3BarChart;
```

Explanation:

We use a `ref` (`svgRef`) to access the SVG element.

In the `useEffect` hook, we use D3.js to:

Select the SVG element.

Define scales (x, y) to map data values to visual coordinates.

Create bars using `selectAll`, `data`, `join`, and various attribute setters (`attr`).

Add axes using `axisBottom` and `axisLeft`.

3. Creating Custom Chart Elements

D3.js allows you to create virtually any visual element you can imagine. Here's an example of creating custom markers for a scatter plot:

JavaScript

```
// ... (previous code) ...


svg

  .selectAll('.dot')

  .data(data)

  .join('path')

  .attr('class', 'dot')

                              .attr('d',
d3.symbol().type(d3.symbolStar).size(100)) // Use
a star symbol

        .attr('transform',        (d)        =>
`translate(${x(d.x)},${y(d.y)})`)

  .attr('fill', 'orange');
```

```
// ... (rest of the code) ...
```

Explanation:

We use `d3.symbol()` to create a star-shaped path.

We set the `d` attribute of the path element to the generated path data.

4. Key Considerations

React and D3.js Lifecycles: Understand how React's component lifecycle (mounting, updating, unmounting) interacts with D3.js's data binding and rendering process.

Data Updates: Efficiently update the D3.js visualization when your React component's props or state change.

Performance: Optimize your D3.js code for performance, especially with large datasets or complex visualizations.

Accessibility: Make your custom D3.js charts accessible by using ARIA attributes and keyboard navigation.

Benefits of using D3.js:

Flexibility: Create highly customized and unique visualizations.

Control: Fine-grained control over every aspect of the visualization.

Animations and Transitions: Implement complex animations and transitions.

Large Ecosystem: Leverage D3.js's vast ecosystem of plugins and extensions.

By integrating D3.js into your React projects, you can unlock a new level of creativity and control in your data visualizations.

10.2 Creating Animated Charts with Libraries (Framer Motion, React Spring) - Code examples: animating chart elements with Framer Motion, creating spring animations

1. Installation

You'll need to install either Framer Motion or React Spring:

Bash

```
# For Framer Motion:

npm install framer-motion


# For React Spring:

npm install react-spring
```

2. Animating with Framer Motion

Framer Motion provides a declarative way to animate React components. Here's how you can animate a bar chart:

JavaScript

```
import React from 'react';

import { BarChart, Bar, XAxis, YAxis, CartesianGrid, Tooltip, Legend } from 'recharts';

import { motion } from 'framer-motion';
```

```javascript
const data = [

  { name: 'A', value: 10 },

  { name: 'B', value: 20 },

  { name: 'C', value: 15 },

];


const barVariants = {

  initial: {

    y: 300, // Start below the chart area

    opacity: 0,

  },

  animate: (i) => ({ // 'i' is the index of the
bar

    y: 0,

    opacity: 1,

    transition: {

      duration: 0.8,

      delay: i * 0.2, // Stagger the animation

    },

  }),

};
```

```
function MyAnimatedBarChart() {

  return (

        <BarChart   width={600}   height={300}
data={data}>

      {/* ... other chart components ... */}

      <Bar dataKey="value" fill="steelblue">

        {data.map((entry, index) => (

          <motion.rect

            key={`bar-${index}`}

            variants={barVariants}

            initial="initial"

            animate="animate"

            custom={index} // Pass the index for
staggered animation

            x={0} // Reset x position for proper
animation

            width="100%" // Make sure the bar
fills the space

          />

        ))}

      </Bar>
```

```
    </BarChart>

  );

}


export default MyAnimatedBarChart;
```

Explanation:

We wrap each bar (`<rect>`) with `motion.rect` from Framer Motion.

`barVariants` defines the animation states (`initial`, `animate`).

`initial="initial"` and `animate="animate"` apply the variants.

`custom={index}` passes the index to the `animate` variant to create a staggered animation.

We reset the `x` and `width` attributes to ensure the bars animate correctly within the chart.

3. Creating Spring Animations with React Spring

React Spring excels at creating spring-based physics animations. Here's how to create a simple spring animation for a line chart:

JavaScript

```
import React, { useState, useEffect } from
'react';

import { LineChart, Line, XAxis, YAxis } from
'recharts';
```

```jsx
import { useSpring, animated } from
'react-spring';


const data = [ /* ... your data ... */ ];


function MySpringLineChart() {

    const [showChart, setShowChart] =
useState(false);

  const springProps = useSpring({

    opacity: showChart ? 1 : 0,

    transform: showChart ? 'translateY(0)' :
'translateY(50px)',

    config: { mass: 1, tension: 180, friction: 12
}, // Spring physics

  });


  useEffect(() => {

    // Simulate data loading or some event to
trigger the animation

    const timer = setTimeout(() => {

      setShowChart(true);

    }, 500);

    return () => clearTimeout(timer);
```

```
    }, []);


    return (

        <animated.div style={springProps}> {/* Apply
spring animation to the chart */}

            <LineChart width={600} height={300}
data={data}>

        {/* ... chart components ... */}

        </LineChart>

    </animated.div>

    );

}


export default MySpringLineChart;
```

Explanation:

We use `useSpring` to create a spring animation with properties for `opacity` and `transform`.

`config` controls the spring physics (mass, tension, friction).

We wrap the `<LineChart>` with `animated.div` to apply the spring animation.

`showChart` state triggers the animation when it becomes `true`.

Key Considerations:

Performance: Be mindful of performance when using animations, especially with large datasets.

Accessibility: Ensure animations are accessible and don't cause distractions or seizures.

User Experience: Use animations thoughtfully to enhance the user experience.

Library Choice: Choose the library (Framer Motion or React Spring) that best suits your needs and animation style.

By incorporating these animation libraries into your Recharts projects, you can create more visually engaging and dynamic data visualizations.

10.3 Building Reusable Chart Components (Creating a library of custom chart components) - Code examples: building a reusable bar chart component, creating a chart component library

Creating a library of reusable chart components can significantly speed up your development process and improve consistency across your projects. Here's how to do it with Recharts:

1. Building a Reusable Bar Chart Component

JavaScript

```javascript
// MyBarChart.js

import React from 'react';

import { BarChart, Bar, XAxis, YAxis, CartesianGrid, Tooltip, Legend } from 'recharts';
```

```jsx
function MyBarChart({ data, title, xDataKey,
yDataKey, barColor }) {

  return (

    <div>

      <h3>{title}</h3>

            <BarChart width={600} height={300}
data={data}>

          <XAxis dataKey={xDataKey} />

          <YAxis />

          <CartesianGrid stroke="#f5f5f5" />

          <Tooltip />

          <Legend />

          <Bar dataKey={yDataKey} fill={barColor}
/>

      </BarChart>

    </div>

  );

}


MyBarChart.defaultProps = {

  title: 'Bar Chart',
```

```
  xDataKey: 'name',

  yDataKey: 'value',

  barColor: '#8884d8',

};
```

```
export default MyBarChart;
```

Explanation:

We create a functional component `MyBarChart` that accepts props for data, title, data keys, and bar color.

This allows you to customize the chart by passing different props.

We set default props for flexibility.

2. Creating a Chart Component Library

Create a new project: Use `create-react-app` or a similar tool to create a new React project for your chart library.

Organize components: Create a folder (e.g., `src/components`) to store your reusable chart components.

Build components: Create reusable components for different chart types (line, pie, area, etc.) following the example above.

Add a build script: Configure a build script (e.g., using `npm run build`) to bundle your library into a distributable format (e.g., a single JavaScript file or a set of modules).

Publish (optional): Publish your library to npm or a private registry to make it easily accessible to other projects.

3. Using the Chart Library

Install the library: In your main project, install your chart library from npm or your registry.

Import components: Import the desired chart components from your library.

JavaScript

```javascript
import React from 'react';

import { MyBarChart, MyLineChart } from 'my-chart-library';          //          Assuming
'my-chart-library' is your library's name


function App() {

   const barChartData = [ /* ... your bar chart
data ... */ ];

   const lineChartData = [ /* ... your line chart
data ... */ ];


   return (

     <div>

            <MyBarChart    data={barChartData}
title="Sales by Category" />

       <MyLineChart data={lineChartData} />

     </div>

   );
```

}

4. Key Considerations

Naming Conventions: Use clear and consistent naming conventions for your components and props.

Documentation: Provide clear documentation for your chart components, including prop descriptions and usage examples.

Testing: Write unit tests for your reusable components to ensure they are working correctly.

Versioning: Use semantic versioning to track changes and ensure compatibility with other projects.

Styling: Consider providing styling options or themes for your charts.

Benefits of Reusable Chart Components:

Efficiency: Reduce development time by reusing components.

Consistency: Maintain a consistent look and feel across your applications.

Maintainability: Update charts in a single place.

Collaboration: Share chart components with other developers.

By creating a library of reusable chart components with Recharts, you can streamline your data visualization workflow and build more efficient and maintainable applications.